CHRISTMAS

Christmas Recipes from Around the World

HOLIDAY RECIPES & MORE

BARBOUR
PUBLISHING

Published by Barbour Publishing, Inc., P.O. Box 719, Uhrichsville, Ohio 44683, www.barbourbooks.com

Our mission is to publish and distribute inspirational products offering exceptional value and biblical encouragement to the masses.

Member of the
Evangelical Christian
Publishers Association

Printed in the United States of America.

Contents

Let's Drink to World Peace!

Good news from heaven the angels bring,
Glad tiding to the earth they sing:
To us this day a child is given,
To crown us with the joy of heaven.

MARTIN LUTHER

Evergreen Punch

2 cups sugar
2 envelopes unsweetened
  lime drink mix

1 (2 liter) bottle ginger ale
2 quarts water
1 (46 ounce) can pineapple
  juice

Combine all ingredients and mix well. Chill and serve.

Julenisse Punch

2 cups sugar
2 cups water
8 cups cranberry juice
3 cups lemon juice

4 cups orange juice
4 cups pineapple juice
1 (2 liter) bottle ginger ale

In a saucepan, combine the sugar and water. Heat, stirring, until sugar is dissolved. Bring to a boil and reduce heat. Cover; cook for 5 minutes without stirring. Add fruit juices; chill. Put ice in punch bowl, pour punch over ice, and add ginger ale.

Polynesian Punch

1½ cups apricot nectar
2½ cups orange juice
1½ cups papaya concentrate
½ cup lemon juice

1 cup sugar
1 (2 liter) bottle ginger ale
1 (17 ounce) can fruit cocktail

In a large pitcher, combine apricot nectar, orange juice, papaya concentrate, lemon juice, and sugar. Stir well. Let stand 1 hour. When ready to serve, pour the liquid into a punch bowl; add ginger ale. Add a block or ring of ice to the bowl. Drain the fruit cocktail; add to punch.

Egghog

⅓ cup sugar
2 egg yolks
⅓ teaspoon salt
4 cups milk
2 egg whites

3 tablespoons sugar
1 teaspoon vanilla
Nutmeg to taste
½ cup whipped topping

Beat ⅓ cup sugar into egg yolks. Add salt and milk. Cook over medium heat, stirring constantly, until mixture coats the spoon. Cool. Beat egg whites until foamy. Gradually add 3 tablespoons sugar, beating into soft peaks. Add vanilla and nutmeg; add to custard mixture and mix thoroughly. Add whipped topping and put some on top to float.

Swedish Wassail

1 gallon apple cider
1 pint water, boiled with 6 small tea bags
1 quart pineapple juice
1 (12 ounce) can frozen orange juice
½ cup sugar

In cloth bag, combine:
2 cinnamon sticks
½ teaspoon whole cloves
1 teaspoon whole allspice

Combine first 5 ingredients in a large pot; add cloth bag ingredients. Simmer for 2 hours, uncovered. Serve hot.

Cranberry Tea

4 cups or 1 pound fresh cranberries
30 cloves
2½ quarts water, divided
2 scant cups sugar
1 cup orange juice

Cook cranberries and cloves in 2 quarts water until cranberries pop; strain. Save juice and discard cranberries and cloves. Dissolve sugar in 2 cups water and add to cranberry juice. Stir in orange juice. Serve hot. Serves 12.

Russian Tea

16 cups water
10 tea bags
3 cinnamon sticks
2 teaspoons whole cloves
2 cups sugar
1 cup lemon juice
1 (46 ounce) can pineapple juice
1 (6 ounce) can frozen orange juice concentrate

In a large saucepan, boil water, tea bags, cinnamon sticks, and cloves. Steep for 15 minutes. Add sugar and juices. Serve hot or cold.

Swedish Egg Coffee

10 to 12 cups water
1 cup regular-grind coffee
1 egg
1 cup ice-cold water

In a saucepan, bring water to a boil and remove from heat. In a small bowl, mix coffee and egg. Add a little hot water to coffee and egg mixture; pour mixture into hot water. Stir and heat until it comes to a rolling boil. Remove from heat and pour in ice-cold water. Let sit 10 minutes before serving. The egg and grounds settle to the bottom, leaving the coffee a dark honey color.

French Chocolate

½ cup semisweet chocolate pieces
½ cup white corn syrup
¼ cup water

1 teaspoon vanilla
1 pint whipping cream
2 quarts milk

In a saucepan, blend chocolate, corn syrup, and water; heat over low heat until melted. Pour into a cup and refrigerate until cool. Add vanilla. In a large bowl, whip cream at medium speed, then gradually add chocolate mixture. Continue beating until mixture mounds. Spoon into a punch bowl and chill. Scald the milk, and pour it into a heated coffee pot. Spoon about 2 tablespoons of the chocolate cream mixture into each cup and pour hot milk over chocolate. Stir. Serves 16.

Far East Spiced Tea

1 gallon boiling water
1 teaspoon cinnamon
3 cloves
3 small tea bags
1½ cups sugar
1 small can frozen orange juice
1 small can frozen lemon juice

In a saucepan, combine water, cinnamon, cloves, and tea bags; boil for 2 minutes. Remove from heat. Add the sugar; stir until dissolved. Strain, then add fruit juices. Bring to a boil, stirring occasionally.

Breads and *Amuse-Bouches*: Tiny Bites to Delight

Christmas Day is a day of joy and charity.
May God make you very rich in both.

PHILLIPS BROOKS

Crab-Filled Lace-Capped Mushrooms

12 to 14 medium mushrooms
⅓ cup butter or margarine, melted
¼ cup cracker crumbs
¼ cup Swiss cheese, shredded
½ teaspoon marjoram
⅛ teaspoon pepper
1 clove garlic, minced
1 (6 ounce) can crab meat

Preheat oven to 375 degrees. Remove stems from mushrooms. Brush caps of mushrooms with melted butter and place, rounded side down, on ungreased baking sheet. Mix the remaining ingredients; spoon into each mushroom cap. Bake for 5 minutes, then broil 6 inches from heat until golden brown.

Tomato-Basil Squares

⅔ cup mayonnaise
1 teaspoon dried basil
1 garlic clove, pressed
2 cups pizza cheese (mozzarella, Parmesan, etc.), divided
1 (10 ounce) package refrigerated pizza crust
4 plum tomatoes, thinly sliced

In a bowl, combine mayonnaise, basil, garlic, and 1 cup of the cheese; mix well.
Roll pizza crust onto a 12x15-inch baking stone and sprinkle crust with 1 cup of
cheese. Arrange tomatoes in a single layer over the layer of cheese. Top tomatoes
with cheese mixture; spread evenly. Bake at 375 degrees for 15 to 20 minutes, or
until top is golden and bubbly. Serve warm; cut with pizza cutter. Serves 20.

Olive and Cheese Ball

1 (8 ounce) package cream cheese or Roquefort cheese, crumbled
½ cup butter or margarine, softened
⅔ cup well-drained and chopped stuffed olives
⅓ cup slivered olives
1 cup almonds, chopped

Blend cheese and butter. Mix in olives. Chill slightly, about 15 minutes. Shape into ball or desired shaped and roll in almonds. Wrap in plastic wrap and chill. Serve on tray with assorted crackers.

Spinach Spread

1 cup mayonnaise
1 cup sour cream
1 package vegetable soup mix
1 cup water chestnuts, cut into small pieces
1 (10 ounce) package frozen spinach, thawed and drained
1 round loaf of bread

Combine first 5 ingredients 1 day ahead and refrigerate. Cut bread by slicing off top. Scoop out inside and cube bread. Fill hollowed loaf with dip and arrange bread cubes around loaf on serving platter. Serves 6.

Avocado Dip

3 avocados, peeled and cubed
2 (8 ounce) packages cream cheese, softened
16 ounces sour cream
1 package taco seasoning mix
1 medium onion, chopped
2 tomatoes, chopped
½ head lettuce, shredded
8 ounces cheddar cheese, shredded
Tortilla chips or cheese-coated chips

Blend peeled and cubed avocados with cream cheese and sour cream until smooth.
Spread as a crust on a round dish, about ½-inch thick. Sprinkle with seasoning
mix, chopped onion, tomatoes, lettuce, and shredded cheese. Serve with chips.

Boursin

1 (8 ounce) package cream cheese, room temperature
½ cup butter, room temperature
¼ teaspoon thyme
¼ teaspoon tarragon
¼ teaspoon basil
¼ teaspoon oregano
¼ teaspoon marjoram
2 cloves garlic, crushed

Combine all ingredients with mixer. Refrigerate for a few days before serving. Serve on water crackers or thinly sliced French bread.

Hot Crab Meat Spread

1 (8 ounce) package cream cheese, softened
¼ cup mayonnaise
1 (8 to 10 ounce) can crab meat
1 tablespoon lemon juice
2 tablespoons Worcestershire sauce
1 bag slivered almonds, divided

Mix all ingredients together, reserving half the bag of nuts; put in 8-inch baking pan. Sprinkle remaining nuts on top. Bake at 350 degrees for 20 minutes. Serve hot with crackers. Serves 15.

Salmon Log

1 (15½ ounce) can red or pink salmon, drained and flaked
1 (8 ounce) package cream cheese, softened
1 tablespoon lemon juice
2 teaspoons minced onion
1 teaspoon horseradish
¼ teaspoon salt
½ teaspoon liquid smoke
½ cup pecans, chopped
3 tablespoons chopped parsley

Combine all ingredients, except pecans and parsley. Chill thoroughly and shape into a 12-inch log. Coat with pecans and parsley. Serve with crackers.

Pineapple Cream Cheese Ball

2 (8 ounce) packages cream cheese, softened
1 small can crushed pineapple, drained
1 (3 ounce) box instant vanilla pudding mix
1 cup walnuts or pecans, chopped

Mix together cream cheese, pineapple, and pudding mix. Shape into ball and roll in walnuts or pecans. Serve with cinnamon graham crackers.

Christmas Wreath Appetizer

1 (8½ ounce) can crushed pineapple
2 (8 ounce) packages cream cheese, softened
¼ cup green bell pepper, finely chopped
4 tablespoons onion, chopped
1 tablespoon seasoned salt
1 to 1½ cups chopped pecans
Parsley, fresh or dried
Whole pimiento

Drain pineapple and add to cream cheese, pepper, onion, salt, and pecans. Mix well and refrigerate until firm. Shape into a "Christmas wreath," sprinkle parsley on top, and add a red "bow" made out of pimiento slices. Serve with assorted crackers.

British Columbia Rolls

2 tablespoons yeast
1¼ cups high-gluten flour
4 cups warm water
½ cup sugar

4 eggs
¾ cup oil
2 teaspoons salt
7 cups high-gluten flour

Mix yeast with 1¼ cups flour. Mix together the next 5 ingredients; add to yeast mixture. Add 7 cups flour (up to 1 cup more, if needed). Knead until smooth and elastic; let rise until double. Punch down and shape. Put in greased pan; let rise 30 minutes. Bake at 350 degrees for 20 minutes. Makes approximately 3 dozen rolls.

Braided French Bread

2 tablespoons yeast
½ cup warm water
1½ cups lukewarm milk
¼ cup sugar
1 tablespoon salt
3 eggs

¼ cup butter, softened
7¼ cups flour
2 egg yolks
2 tablespoons water
Sesame seeds

In a large bowl, dissolve yeast in water. Stir in milk, sugar, and salt. Add eggs, butter, and gradually add flour (add ¼ cup more, if needed), kneading until smooth, about 5 minutes. Round up in greased bowl; bring greased side up. Cover and let rise in warm place until double, approximately 1½ to 2 hours. Punch down; let rise 30 minutes. Divide dough into 6 parts, forming six 14-inch rolls. Braid 3 rolls; loosely fasten at ends. Place on ungreased baking sheet. Let rise 1 hour. Brush braids with egg yolks and 2 tablespoons water. Sprinkle with sesame seeds. Bake at 350 degrees for 25 minutes; cover with plastic wrap to cool.

Angel Biscuits

1 package dry yeast
2 tablespoons warm water
2 cups buttermilk
5 cups flour
½ cup sugar

1 tablespoon baking powder
1 teaspoon salt
1 teaspoon baking soda
1 cup shortening

Combine yeast and water; set aside for 5 minutes. Add buttermilk, set aside. In another bowl, combine dry ingredients; cut in shortening. Add buttermilk and yeast mixture. Use fork to mix until dry ingredients are moistened. Place on a floured board; knead 3 to 4 times. Roll, cut, and bake on greased pan at 400 degrees for 10 to 12 minutes.

*Note: After kneading, the dough may be stored, covered, in the refrigerator for 4 to 5 days. Roll, cut, and bake.

Cheese Biscuits

2 cups sifted flour
3 teaspoons baking powder
½ teaspoon salt
¼ cup shortening
½ cup Swiss or cheddar
  cheese, grated

⅔ cup milk
1 egg, slightly beaten
2 to 3 tablespoons butter,
  melted

Sift dry ingredients together. Cut in shortening and cheese, mixing well. Add milk and egg, stirring quickly until soft dough is formed. Turn onto lightly floured surface and knead into smooth ball. Roll lightly to 2-inch thickness and cut with floured biscuit cutter. Bake on ungreased cookie sheet at 375 degrees for 12 to 15 minutes. Brush with melted butter immediately after removing from oven.

Sweet Potato Biscuits

4 cups flour
⅔ cup sugar
2 tablespoons baking powder
1½ teaspoons salt
2 cups sweet potatoes, warm, cooked, and mashed
½ cup oil or shortening
¼ cup milk

Mix all ingredients together. Roll into average-size biscuits. Bake on greased pan at 475 degrees for 15 minutes. Makes 36 rolls.

Dill Bread

1 cup cottage cheese
1 package yeast
¼ cup warm water
1 teaspoon sugar
1 tablespoon minced onion
1 tablespoon butter

1 teaspoon dill seed
1 teaspoon salt
¼ teaspoon baking soda
1 egg, unbeaten
2¼ to 2½ cups flour

Warm cottage cheese. Dissolve yeast in water. Add the remaining ingredients except flour. Add flour; mix. No kneading necessary. Place in 2 well-greased bread pans. Bake at 350 degrees for 30 minutes. Cover and bake 15 minutes longer.

Christmas Braid

½ cup butter
1½ cups buttermilk
2 packages yeast
½ cup sugar
½ teaspoon salt
4 cups flour

½ cup strawberry jam
1 egg, beaten
½ cup powdered sugar
1 tablespoon water
Candied cherries

In a medium saucepan, heat butter and buttermilk to melt butter. Pour into large bowl and cool to 105 to 115 degrees. Sprinkle yeast over warm buttermilk once it is at temperature. Stir to dissolve. Add sugar, salt, and half of the flour. Beat at medium speed until smooth. With wooden spoon or pastry hooks of mixer, add remaining flour. Knead by hand or machine 5 minutes. Place in lightly greased bowl. Cover and let rise 45 to 60 minutes. Knead again until smooth. Separate into 3 balls. Roll each into a rectangle, about 15 inches long. Spread one-third of the jam in center of each rectangle. Transfer rectangles to baking sheets or 9x13-inch pan. Make diagonal slits down each side of rectangle, each about 4 inches long. Fold each flap in alternately, over jam, to make braided appearance. Let rise another hour or until desired size. Brush with beaten egg and bake at 375 degrees for 20 to 25 minutes. Cool and decorate with powdered sugar and water, mixed to glaze. Decorate over icing with candied cherries to look like holly and berries. Makes three 15-inch braids.

Onion Herb Bread

½ cup butter or margarine
2 tablespoons minced onion or instant onion flakes
1 tablespoon prepared mustard
2 tablespoons lemon juice
1 teaspoon seasoning salt
1 tablespoon poppyseed
Loaf of French bread or petit French rolls
Slices of jack cheese

Mix together the first 6 ingredients. Slice bread lengthwise, cutting from top to bottom but not all the way through. Insert cheese into the slices. Place herb mixture on top of loaf, or spread on the rolls. Wrap in foil (if petit rolls, wrap each individually). Bake at 350 degrees for 25 to 30 minutes. Serve immediately.

South African Overnight Bread

2 cakes compressed yeast or
  2 packages dry yeast
2½ quarts water
3 cups sugar
2 cups butter or margarine

1 (14 ounce) can sweetened
  condensed milk
2 teaspoons salt
10 cups flour
4 eggs, well beaten

In a saucepan, mix together and heat the yeast, water, sugar, butter, and condensed milk. In a large bowl, combine the salt and flour; add the eggs and milk mixture and knead well. Cover and let rise in a warm place overnight. Form into balls and place on baking pans. Cover and let rise well again. Bake at 375 degrees for 45 minutes.

Delectable Salads and Sides

I will honor Christmas in my heart,
and try to keep it all the year.

CHARLES DICKENS

Holiday Yams

1 (16 ounce) can sliced peaches
1 tablespoon cornstarch
⅓ cup liquid brown sugar
1 (8 ounce) can whole cranberry sauce
½ teaspoon cinnamon
2 tablespoons butter
1 (17 ounce) can yams, drained

Drain peaches; reserve juice. Dissolve cornstarch in ¼ cup peach juice; set aside. In a skillet, heat remaining juice, brown sugar, cranberry sauce, cinnamon, and butter. When butter is melted, add cornstarch mixture, stirring until thickened. Add yams; cook 10 minutes. Add peaches and cook 5 minutes more or until heated throughout. Serves 6 to 8.

Oyster Nut Stuffing

1 cup butter
1 cup onion, chopped
1 stalk celery, chopped
9 cups bread crumbs
1 cup finely chopped chestnuts

½ cup white cooking wine
2 tablespoons chopped parsley
2 teaspoons salt
½ teaspoon white pepper
25 oysters in liquid

In a saucepan, melt butter and sauté onion and celery until golden. Stir in bread crumbs. Add nuts and moisten with wine to make a paste. Add seasonings. Drain oysters and heat liquid to boiling in a separate saucepan. Cut oysters in half and add to hot liquid, cooking until edges curl. Drain and add oysters to stuffing mixture. This will make enough to stuff a 12- to 15-pound turkey.

Scalloped Oysters

½ cup bread crumbs
1 cup cracker crumbs
½ cup butter or margarine,
    melted
1 pint oysters, drained; reserve liquid

Salt to taste
Pepper to taste
¼ cup oyster liquid
2 tablespoons cream

Mix bread crumbs and cracker crumbs with melted butter. Sprinkle a thin layer of crumbs in the bottom of a shallow, greased 9x13-inch baking dish. Cover with oysters; sprinkle with salt and pepper. Add half of the oyster liquid and half of the cream. Repeat to make a second layer. Cover with remaining crumbs. Bake for 30 minutes at 425 degrees in covered baking dish.

German Potato Bake

9 medium potatoes	2 teaspoons salt
8 slices bacon (more if desired)	½ teaspoon celery seed
¾ cup chopped onion	¾ cup water
2 tablespoons sugar	⅓ cup vinegar (scant)
2 tablespoons flour	

Cook potatoes; slice or dice and place in 9x13-inch baking dish. Fry bacon until crisp; remove from skillet. Crumble bacon over potatoes. Fry the onion in the bacon drippings until golden brown. Blend in sugar, flour, salt, and celery seed. Cook over low heat, stirring until it boils. Remove from heat; stir in water and vinegar. Return to heat and cook until boiling, stirring constantly. Boil for 1 minute. Pour over potatoes and bacon; gently toss. Bake at 350 degrees for 1 hour. Can be made a day or two in advance and kept in refrigerator until ready to bake.

Baked Winter Squash

6 cups winter squash, mashed
⅓ cup butter or margarine, melted
6 eggs, beaten

½ cup sugar
½ teaspoon salt

Topping:
1 cup brown sugar
¼ cup butter or margarine,
  softened

¼ cup flour
¼ cup oatmeal
½ cup almonds

Combine first 5 ingredients; place in ungreased 9x13-inch baking dish. Combine topping ingredients and crumble over the top. Bake uncovered at 350 degrees for 45 minutes. Serves 12.

Christmas Salad

2 small boxes lime gelatin
2 cups hot water

¼ cup cold water
2 cups crushed pineapple

Middle filling:
2 (3 ounce) packages cream cheese
⅓ cup salad dressing or mayonnaise

½ cup walnuts

Top layer:
1 small box cherry gelatin
1 cup hot water

¼ cup cold water
1 tablespoon lemon juice

Combine first 4 ingredients; pour into attractive glass bowl and chill until set. Mix together middle filling and layer on top of lime gelatin mixture; chill until set. For top layer, combine gelatin and water; let cool. Add lemon juice. Pour on top of cream cheese layer; chill until set.

Baked Pineapple

½ cup butter, softened
1¾ cups sugar
3 eggs, beaten
4 cups bread, cubed
1 (20 ounce) can crushed pineapple
½ cup milk

Preheat oven to 350 degrees. In a large bowl, cream butter and sugar. Add eggs; stir in bread cubes and pineapple. Add milk. Put in a greased 2-quart casserole dish and bake for 1 hour.

Pineapple Sweet Potatoes

½ tablespoon butter or margarine
1 (8 ounce) can crushed pineapple and juice
2 cups fresh sweet potatoes, cooked and sliced
¼ teaspoon cinnamon
⅛ teaspoon salt, optional

Heat butter in large frying pan. Add pineapple and sweet potatoes. Sprinkle with cinnamon and salt. Simmer, uncovered, until most of the juice has cooked away, 10 to 15 minutes. Turn potatoes and coat with juice, then serve.

Make-Ahead Mashed Potatoes

3 pounds medium-size potatoes,
  peeled
1½ cups sour cream
4 tablespoons butter or margarine
1½ teaspoons salt

¼ teaspoon pepper
¼ cup bread crumbs
1 tablespoon butter or
  margarine, melted

Cook potatoes to boiling in salted water until tender. Drain well. In a large bowl, combine potatoes, sour cream, 4 tablespoons butter, and seasonings. Beat at low speed until blended; beat at high speed until light and fluffy. Spoon into lightly greased 2-quart casserole dish. Cover and refrigerate overnight. Bake, covered, at 325 degrees for 1 hour. Mix bread crumbs with melted butter. Sprinkle over potatoes. Continue baking uncovered 30 minutes.

Cheese Scalloped Carrots

12 medium carrots, pared and sliced
¼ cup butter or margarine
1 small onion, minced
¼ cup flour
1 teaspoon salt
¼ teaspoon dry mustard

2 cups milk
⅛ teaspoon pepper
¼ teaspoon celery salt
½ pound sharp cheddar
    cheese, shredded
3 cups buttered fresh bread
    crumbs

Cook carrots in boiling salted water; drain. Meanwhile, in butter in saucepan, gently cook onion 2 to 3 minutes. Stir in flour, salt, mustard, and milk; cook, stirring until smooth. Add pepper and celery salt. In a 2-quart casserole dish, arrange layers of carrots, then layer of cheese. Repeat until both are used, ending with carrots. Pour on sauce; top with crumbs. Bake, uncovered, at 350 degrees for 25 minutes, until golden. Serves 8.

   *If making early in the day, refrigerate. To serve, bake uncovered at 350 degrees for 35 to 45 minutes, or until hot.

Baked Sweet Potatoes

3 cups sweet potatoes, mashed
½ cup sugar
½ cup butter

2 eggs, beaten
1 teaspoon vanilla
⅓ cup milk

Topping:
⅓ cup butter, melted
1 cup light brown sugar

½ cup flour
1 cup pecans

In a large bowl, mix together sweet potatoes, sugar, butter, eggs, vanilla, and milk. Spread in 9x13-inch baking dish. Mix together topping ingredients and sprinkle over potato mixture. Bake at 350 degrees for 25 minutes.

Curried Rice

½ cup butter
1 small onion, finely chopped
1 teaspoon curry powder

2¼ to 2½ cups water
1 cup converted rice

In a 1½-quart saucepan, melt the butter; add the onion and cook fairly quickly, stirring often, until golden. Stir in the curry powder and the water; bring to a boil. Add the rice and cook over very low heat. Cover tightly until rice is tender, about 20 minutes. Remove from heat; let stand, tightly covered, about 5 minutes. Makes 6 servings.

Marinated Mushroom-Spinach Salad

½ cup oil
¼ cup white wine vinegar
1 small onion, sliced
½ teaspoon basil
1 teaspoon salt

¾ teaspoon fresh ground
  pepper
½ pound mushrooms,
  washed and sliced thin
1 pound spinach, washed and
  torn into bite-size pieces

In a medium bowl, combine oil, vinegar, onion, basil, salt, and pepper. Add mushrooms. Let stand at room temperature for 2 hours or refrigerate overnight, stirring occasionally. Place spinach in salad bowl; add mushroom-oil mixture and toss well. Serve at once. Serves 6.

Cranberry Cream Salad

2 packages cherry-flavored gelatin
2 cups hot water

1 can jellied cranberry sauce
  (not whole)
2 cups sour cream

Dissolve gelatin in hot water. Chill until partially set. Fold in cranberry sauce and sour cream. Spoon into mold and chill. Serves 8 to 10.

Copper Carrot Pennies

2 pounds carrots, sliced
1 small green pepper
1 medium onion
1 can tomato soup
½ cup vegetable or canola oil

1 cup sugar
¾ cup vinegar
1 teaspoon prepared mustard
1 teaspoon Worcestershire
  sauce
Salt and pepper to taste

Slice carrots in even disks. Slice green pepper in rings. Slice onion thinly. Boil carrots until crisp-tender. Alternate layers of carrots, green pepper rings, and onion slices in baking dish. Combine remaining ingredients and beat until smooth. Pour over vegetables. Refrigerate. Serve cold.

Evergreen Gelatin Salad

1 large box lime gelatin
2 cups boiling water
1 (8 ounce) package cream
  cheese

1 (15 ounce) can crushed
  pineapple
1 (12 ounce) container
  whipped topping

Combine gelatin and boiling water; allow to cool. Combine cream cheese, pineapple, and whipped topping. Add to gelatin mixture. Chill until firm. Serves 12.

Cranberry Waldorf Salad

3 (3 ounce) packages peach gelatin
1¼ teaspoons salt
3 cups boiling water
2 cups cranberry juice cocktail

2 tablespoons lemon juice
1½ cups apples, diced
½ cup nuts, coarsely chopped

Dissolve gelatin and salt in boiling water. Stir in cranberry juice and lemon juice. Chill until slightly thickened. Fold in apples and nuts. Chill until firm. Can be put into a 2-quart mold.

Cauliflower Salad

4 cups raw cauliflower florets
1 cup stuffed green olives, chopped
⅔ cup green pepper, chopped
½ cup onion, chopped
½ cup pimiento (may include
    ones in stuffed olives)

½ cup salad oil
3 tablespoons lemon juice
3 tablespoons wine vinegar
1 tablespoon salt
½ teaspoon sugar
¼ teaspoon pepper

Combine cauliflower, olives, green pepper, onion, and pimiento. Shake remaining ingredients together to make a dressing, and pour over vegetables. Refrigerate 4 hours.

Greek Salad

2 heads Boston lettuce, torn
4 ounces feta cheese, crumbled
18 to 20 Greek calamata olives
6 Roma tomatoes, quartered

6 green onions, chopped
3 stalks celery, chopped
1 green pepper, chopped
1 box croutons (optional)

Vinaigrette Dressing:
1 clove garlic, minced
¾ cup olive oil
¼ cup red wine vinegar
1 teaspoon salt
¼ teaspoon pepper

¼ teaspoon paprika
¼ teaspoon oregano
½ teaspoon sugar
1 tablespoon Dijon mustard
   or 1 teaspoon dry mustard

Toss lettuce with remaining salad ingredients. Garnish with Vinaigrette Dressing: Marinate garlic in oil for 1 hour. Add remaining ingredients and shake well. Chill. Serves 6.

Orange Almond Salad with Romaine Lettuce

1 head romaine lettuce, torn
1 (15 ounce) can mandarin
  oranges, drained

2 tablespoons sesame seeds,
  toasted
2 kiwifruit, sliced (optional)
Slivered almonds

Dressing:
2 tablespoons white wine vinegar
¼ cup salad oil
2 tablespoons sugar

½ teaspoon salt
⅛ teaspoon almond extract
Dash pepper

Toss together all salad ingredients. Mix dressing ingredients and combine with salad.

Pea Salad

2 packages frozen tiny peas, thawed and drained
6 slices bacon, fried and crumbled, or ¼ cup bacon bits
1 cup sour cream
3 green onions, sliced
½ cup salted peanuts

Mix all ingredients together except peanuts. Add peanuts just before serving so they won't get soggy.

Cream-Style Corn Pudding

2 (14¾ ounce) cans cream-style corn
4 eggs, beaten
½ cup butter, melted
½ cup sugar
2 heaping tablespoons flour
Dash cinnamon
Dash nutmeg

Preheat oven to 350 degrees. Mix all ingredients except cinnamon and nutmeg. Sprinkle those on top. Bake for 1 hour or until puffed up in the center.

Italian Green Beans Amandine

3 tablespoons butter
¼ cup blanched slivered almonds
2 (9 ounce) packages frozen Italian green beans
½ teaspoon seasoned salt

Melt butter in a skillet over low heat. Add almonds and stir until browned. Add frozen beans and salt; cover and cook for 5 minutes, separating beans with a fork as they thaw. Heat and stir, uncovered, for 8 to 10 minutes or until water is evaporated and beans are tender and crisp.

Spinach-Stuffed Tomatoes

1 (10 ounce) package frozen
  chopped spinach
¼ cup water
¼ cup mayonnaise

1 tablespoon dried minced
  onion
⅛ teaspoon nutmeg
Salt and pepper to taste
6 small whole tomatoes

Cook spinach in water for 3 minutes, stirring to defrost; drain completely. Combine spinach with mayonnaise, onion, nutmeg, salt, and pepper. Cut a thin slice off the top of tomatoes and scoop out the center; drain upside down. Sprinkle inside of tomatoes with salt and fill with spinach mixture. Place tomatoes in a baking dish and pour hot water ¼ inch deep around tomatoes. Bake at 350 degrees for 12 to 15 minutes. Serves 6.

French Rice

1 (10¾ ounce) can onion soup,
   undiluted
½ cup butter or margarine, melted
1 (4½ ounce) jar sliced mushrooms

1 (8 ounce) can sliced water
   chestnuts
1 cup uncooked rice

Preheat oven to 350 degrees. In a large bowl, combine soup and butter. Drain mushrooms and water chestnuts, reserving liquid. Add enough water to reserved liquid to equal 1⅓ cups. Add mushrooms, water chestnuts, liquid, and rice to soup mixture; stir well. Pour into a lightly greased 10x6x2-inch baking dish. Cover and bake for 1 hour. Serves 6.

Almond Raisin Pilaf

½ cup onion, chopped
2 tablespoons butter or margarine
2 tablespoons olive oil
1 cup converted rice
½ cup slivered almonds
2½ cups chicken broth
1½ teaspoons salt

¼ teaspoon pepper
⅓ cup golden raisins
2 tablespoons fresh chopped
  parsley
1½ teaspoons fresh chopped
  mint leaves

In a medium saucepan, cook onion in butter and oil until tender, approximately 5 minutes. Add rice and almonds. Stirring constantly, cook over low heat until golden. Add chicken broth, salt, and pepper. Bring to a boil; reduce heat. Cover tightly; simmer for 20 minutes. Stir in remaining ingredients. Remove from heat; let stand, covered, until all liquid is absorbed, approximately 5 minutes. Serves 6.

Intercontinental Centerpieces

For a child is born to us, a son is given to us.
The government will rest on his shoulders. And he will
be called: Wonderful Counselor, Mighty God,
Everlasting Father, Prince of Peace.

ISAIAH 9:6 NLT

Beef with Oyster Sauce

1 pound beef tenderloin, thinly sliced
1½ tablespoons sesame oil
1 tablespoon cornstarch
1 tablespoon soy sauce
3 tablespoons oil
1 teaspoon garlic, minced
2 tablespoons water

1 tablespoon sugar
½ cup straw mushrooms
2 tablespoons oyster sauce
1 cup onion, sliced
3 stalks green onions,
   cut into 1-inch pieces

Mix beef with sesame oil, cornstarch, and soy sauce. Let stand for 30 minutes. Heat oil in a large frying pan. Sauté minced garlic until golden brown. Add beef. Sauté until just done. Add water, sugar, straw mushrooms, oyster sauce, onion, and green onion. Cook 1 more minute.

Grilled Ham with Apricot Sauce

½ cup whole cranberry sauce
¼ cup apricot preserves

½ cup barbecue sauce
1 fully cooked center cut ham slice

Heat grill. In a small bowl, combine the first 3 ingredients. Cut slashes at fat edge of ham to prevent curling. Place ham on gas grill over medium heat. Cook 15 to 25 minutes, turning 2 or 3 times, and brushing with sauce. Top with additional sauce before serving. Makes 6 servings.

Ham with Coke

1 ham
Cloves
1 small can pineapple rings

Brown sugar
Water
1 (12 ounce) can Coke

Place ham in roaster. Stud with cloves. Put pineapple on ham with toothpicks. Put brown sugar in holes of pineapple. Pour water over brown sugar. Bake at 325 degrees for 1 hour. Baste with half can of Coke. Bake another hour and baste with remaining Coke. Bake until done.

Veal in Wine with Mushrooms

3 pounds veal, cut into 1-inch cubes
2 tablespoons butter
2 (4½ ounce) cans mushroom caps
½ cup cooking oil
1 cup white cooking wine

½ cup onions, chopped
1 teaspoon oregano
1 cup sour cream
5⅓ cups cooked rice

Brown veal in butter. Add remaining ingredients except sour cream and rice; simmer 30 to 40 minutes until tender. Remove from heat and add sour cream; serve with cooked rice.

Creamy Chicken and Rice with Thyme

¾ cup chicken broth or water
½ teaspoon salt
1½ cups quick-cooking rice
1½ to 2 pounds split chicken breast
1 (6 ounce) can sliced mushrooms
   with liquid

1 (10½ ounce) can cream of
   mushroom soup
½ teaspoon thyme
1 tablespoon fine bread
   crumbs
1 tablespoon melted butter

In a greased pan, combine the first 3 ingredients. Place chicken over rice mixture. Combine mushrooms and soup. Spread over chicken. Sprinkle with thyme, bread crumbs, and butter. Cover tightly with foil and bake at 400 degrees for 1 hour, or until chicken is done. Serves 4.

Plum-Glazed Chicken

6 plums
¼ cup sugar
¼ cup orange juice
1 teaspoon lemon juice
1 whole chicken breast,
  with bone, halved

Salt to taste
Pepper to taste
Paprika to taste
Hot cooked rice

Slice and pit plums. Place in greased 8x8-inch baking pan. Stir in sugar, orange juice, and lemon juice. Season chicken with salt, pepper, and paprika. Arrange on top of plums, skin side up. Bake at 400 degrees for 40 to 50 minutes. Baste with juice occasionally. Arrange chicken on rice. Spoon plum sauce over all. Serves 2.

Flank Steak Marinade

½ cup soy sauce
¼ cup brown sugar
1 clove garlic, minced,
   or ½ teaspoon garlic powder
2 tablespoons vegetable oil

1 teaspoon ground ginger
½ teaspoon monosodium
   glutamate
Flank steak (approximately
   2 pounds)

For marinade, combine all ingredients except steak. Mix well. Score both sides of steak and place in a glass 9x13-inch baking dish. Spoon the marinade over the steak and let stand for at least 2 hours at room temperature, turning the steak over about every 30 minutes. (Steak can be marinated in the refrigerator but will require approximately 4 hours to achieve the same degree of flavor as at room temperature.) Remove from marinade and broil steak under broiler or grill over coals. Slice steak across the grain and serve. Marinade is also good with chicken, pork chops, or ribs.

Oriental Charcoal Broiled Roast

5 ounces soy sauce
2 cups tomato juice
Juice of 2 lemons

1 tablespoon dehydrated onion
2 to 3 pounds chuck roast,
    cut about 2 inches thick

Combine soy sauce, tomato juice, lemon juice, and onion to make marinade. Marinate roast for several hours or overnight. Grill over hot charcoals; cut into thin slices to serve. Serves 6.

Irish Boiled Dinner

4 pounds corned beef brisket
1 can condensed onion soup
4 whole peppercorns
1 medium clove garlic, minced
1 bay leaf
¼ teaspoon crushed rosemary
6 medium carrots, cut into
   bite-size pieces

7 medium potatoes, quartered
½ cup celery, cut into
   bite-size pieces
1 medium head green cabbage,
   cut into wedges
3 tablespoons water
3 tablespoons flour

Rinse corned beef well. Place in a large heavy pan; add soup and seasonings. Cover and cook over low heat for 3½ hours. Add carrots, potatoes, and celery. Place cabbage on top. Cover and cook about 1 hour or until all ingredients are tender. Remove meat, vegetables, and bay leaf. Gradually blend water into flour until smooth; slowly stir into the sauce in the bottom of the pan. Cook, stirring until thickened. Add meat and vegetables and serve. Serves 8.

Shrimp Newburg

6 tablespoons butter
2 tablespoons flour
1½ cups light cream
3 egg yolks, beaten
2 cups cooked shrimp
2 teaspoons lemon juice

3 tablespoons water or
    chicken broth
¼ teaspoon salt
Paprika to taste
Toast points

In a saucepan, blend butter and flour; add cream all at once. Heat over low heat and stir until thickened. Stir a small amount of hot mixture into yolks, and return to the pan. Cook, stirring, until thick. Add shrimp, then add lemon juice, water or broth, salt, and paprika. Serve with toast points.

Garlic and Rosemary Leg of Lamb

Leg of lamb
Garlic cloves
Salt and pepper

Flour
Dried rosemary
Water

Ask your butcher to bone and tie leg. Push garlic cloves into inside of lamb. Rub salt, pepper, and flour all over the lamb. Place in a roasting pan and sprinkle with dried rosemary. Cook at 350 degrees for 30 minutes per pound of meat. Add water to pan as needed. Remove lamb and make gravy with drippings.

Apricot Chicken

1 whole chicken, cut and cleaned,
or 6 boneless, skinless chicken breasts
1 small jar apricot preserves

1 (ounce) bottle Catalina salad
dressing
1 packet onion soup mix
6 servings cooked white rice

Place chicken in a 9x13-inch baking dish. Combine apricot preserves, Catalina dressing, and dry onion soup mix. Pour mixture over chicken. Cover and bake at 350 degrees for 1 hour. Uncover and bake 30 minutes more or until bubbly. Prepare rice according to package directions and serve with chicken.

Chicken Orange

1 chicken, cut into pieces
Herbs as desired
½ cup butter, melted

1 small can frozen orange
juice concentrate

Remove skin from chicken and arrange pieces in a baking dish. Sprinkle with herbs. Combine melted butter and undiluted orange juice. Pour mixture over chicken and bake at 350 degrees, uncovered, for 1 hour.

Veal à la Basil

8 ounces veal cutlets
½ teaspoon salt
⅛ teaspoon pepper
2 tablespoons lemon juice

½ teaspoon basil
2 tablespoons vinegar
1 tablespoon parsley flakes

Season veal with salt and pepper. Brown meat in pan over high heat, using no fat. Add remaining ingredients. Cover; simmer over low heat until meat is tender, about 6 minutes.

Baked Pork Chops and Apples

4 to 6 apples, peeled and sliced
½ cup brown sugar
2 tablespoons flour

½ teaspoon cinnamon
¼ teaspoon nutmeg
6 pork chops, browned

Mix apples, sugar, flour, and spices; place in oblong baking dish. Top with browned pork chops. Cover and bake 1½ hours at 375 degrees. Serve with the apples and sauce on top of the pork chops.

All Things *Dulce* and Decadent

"They will call him Immanuel"—
which means, "God with us."

Matthew 1:23 niv

Butter Horns

1 cup butter
2 cups sifted flour

1 egg yolk, slightly beaten
¾ cup sour cream

Filling:
¾ cup sugar
¾ cup walnuts, finely chopped

1 teaspoon cinnamon

In a bowl, cut butter into flour. In a separate bowl, combine egg yolk and sour cream; add to flour mixture. Mix well until blended. Form into 3 balls and wrap in waxed paper. Chill overnight. Roll each piece into a 12-inch circle; cut into 16 wedges. Combine filling ingredients and sprinkle on dough. Roll each wedge, beginning with outside edge. Bake at 375 degrees for 15 to 20 minutes.

German Apple Cake

½ cup shortening
½ cup brown sugar
1 cup sugar
2 eggs
2¼ cups cake flour

Topping:
½ cup brown sugar
¼ cup sugar

¼ teaspoon salt
2 teaspoons cinnamon
2 teaspoons baking soda
1 cup sour milk or buttermilk
2 cups apples, diced

½ cup chopped nuts
1 teaspoon cinnamon

In a large bowl, cream shortening, sugars, and eggs. In a separate bowl, sift flour, salt, and cinnamon together. In another bowl, add baking soda to sour milk. Alternately add flour mixture and baking soda mixture to the batter. Fold in apples. Mix the topping ingredients together and sprinkle over the batter. Bake at 350 degrees in a 9x13-inch pan for 35 to 40 minutes.

Snickerdoodles

½ cup shortening
½ cup butter, softened
1½ cups sugar
2 eggs

3 cups flour
2 teaspoons cream of tartar
1 teaspoon baking soda
¼ teaspoon salt

Cinnamon mixture:
2 tablespoons sugar
2 teaspoons cinnamon

In a large bowl, mix shortening, sugar, and eggs. In a separate bowl, combine dry ingredients and add to creamed mixture. Shape dough into 1-inch balls and roll in cinnamon mixture. Bake at 375 degrees for 10 minutes.

Chinese Chews

½ cup butter or margarine
2 tablespoons sugar
1 cup flour
2 eggs
1½ cups brown sugar

1 teaspoon vanilla
¼ cup coconut
¾ cup nuts
2 tablespoons flour

In a medium bowl, mix together butter, sugar, and flour. Press into a 9x13-inch pan and bake at 350 degrees for 15 minutes. Meanwhile, mix together eggs, brown sugar, vanilla, coconut, nuts, and flour. Pour on baked crust; bake another 25 minutes.

Christmas Spice Cookies

¾ cup sugar
⅔ cup butter or margarine,
   softened
¼ cup orange juice
½ cup dark corn syrup
½ cup dark molasses
4½ cups all-purpose flour

¾ cup whole wheat flour
2 teaspoons ginger
1 teaspoon baking soda
1 teaspoon salt
½ teaspoon ground cloves
½ teaspoon nutmeg
½ teaspoon allspice

In a large bowl, cream sugar and butter. Blend in orange juice, corn syrup, and molasses. In a separate bowl, combine flours, ginger, baking soda, salt, cloves, nutmeg, and allspice. Add to creamed mixture; mix well. Chill 3 to 4 hours or overnight. Roll a portion of the dough on a lightly floured surface to ¼-inch thickness. Cut into desired shapes. Place 2 inches apart on greased baking sheets. Repeat with remaining dough. Bake at 350 degrees for 12 to 14 minutes. Makes 6 to 7 dozen.

Black Forest Brownies

1 (3 ounce) package cream
  cheese, softened
1 tablespoon milk
1/3 cup sugar
1 1/3 cups flour
1 1/4 cups sugar
1/2 cup oil
1/4 cup cocoa

2 teaspoons vanilla
1/4 teaspoon salt
3 eggs
1 (21 ounce) can cherry
  pie filling
1 (1 ounce) square semisweet
  chocolate

In a medium bowl, mix first 3 ingredients; set aside. In a large bowl, mix flour, sugar, oil, cocoa, vanilla, salt, and eggs until just blended. Spread in a greased 9x13-inch pan. Drop cream cheese mixture by teaspoonfuls on top and swirl into batter with a knife. Bake at 350 degrees for 20 minutes. Remove from oven and spread pie filling on top. Bake 10 minutes longer. Cool; melt chocolate and drizzle over brownies. Cool; cut into squares.

Sopaipillas

1¾ cups flour
2 teaspoons baking powder
1 teaspoon salt
2 tablespoons shortening

⅔ cup water
Oil for deep-fat frying
Honey

In a bowl, combine the dry ingredients; cut in shortening until crumbly. Gradually add water, tossing with a fork until mixture holds together. On a lightly floured surface, knead dough for 1 to 2 minutes or until smooth. Cover and let stand for 5 minutes. Roll out to ¼-inch thickness. Cut with a 2½-inch star cookie cutter or into 2½-inch triangles.

In an electric skillet or deep-fat fryer, heat oil to 375 degrees. Fry sopaipillas for 1 to 2 minutes on each side or until golden brown and puffed. Drain on paper towels. Serve immediately with honey. Yield: 1 dozen.

Chocolate Soufflé

1 envelope unflavored gelatin
3 tablespoons cold water
2 ounces unsweetened chocolate
½ cup powdered sugar
1 cup milk

½ cup sugar
¼ teaspoon salt
1 teaspoon vanilla
4 cups whipped topping

Dissolve gelatin in cold water; set aside. In a saucepan, melt chocolate over low heat. Stir in powdered sugar as thoroughly as possible. Scald milk and stir into chocolate mixture; cook, stirring constantly, until it reaches the boiling point. Remove from heat and stir in softened gelatin, sugar, salt, and vanilla. Chill until as thick as raw egg whites. Beat until light. Add whipped topping; beat until combined. Chill 2 to 3 hours.

Fried Ice Cream

2 cups ice cream
1 egg, beaten
¼ teaspoon vanilla

2½ cups corn flakes, crushed
½ teaspoon cinnamon
Honey, chocolate syrup, or
crushed strawberries

Make 4 balls with ½ cup ice cream each. Freeze for 1 hour. In a mixing bowl, beat egg and add vanilla. In a pie plate, mix corn flakes and cinnamon. Dip balls in egg mixture, then roll in the crumbs. Freeze for 1 hour, then repeat. Deep fry at 375 degrees for 15 seconds. Serve with honey, chocolate syrup, or crushed strawberries. Serves 4.

Caramel Cream Tarts

2 (3 ounce) packages cream
cheese, softened
1 cup butter or margarine, softened
2 cups flour
1 (14 ounce) bag caramels
½ cup evaporated milk
¼ cup sugar

2 tablespoons + 2 teaspoons
evaporated milk
½ cup butter or margarine,
softened
½ teaspoon vanilla
½ cup walnuts, ground

In a large bowl, mix cream cheese, 1 cup butter, and flour. Mix well to form a ball. Divide into 48 equal pieces. Press dough up to rim in tart pans. Bake at 350 degrees for 15 minutes. Carefully invert shells on rack to cool. Melt caramels in milk and keep warm. Fill cooled shells. Mix sugar, evaporated milk, ½ cup butter, and vanilla. Beat until creamy. Frost tarts and top with nuts. Makes 4 dozen.

Mincemeat Bars

2 cups rolled oats
1¾ cups flour
½ teaspoon baking soda
1 cup brown sugar

1 cup butter or margarine,
   softened
1½ to 2 cups mincemeat

Mix first 5 ingredients together. Put half of crumbs in the bottom of a 9x13-inch pan. Spread mincemeat over top evenly. Cover with remaining crumbs. Bake at 350 degrees for 35 to 40 minutes. Cook and cut into bars.

Caramel Flan

¾ cup sugar
4 eggs
1¾ cups water

1 (14 ounce) can sweetened
condensed milk
½ teaspoon vanilla
⅛ teaspoon salt

In heavy skillet, over medium heat, cook sugar, stirring constantly, until melted and caramel covered. Pour into 9-inch square or round baking pan, tilting to completely coat the bottom. In a medium mixing bowl, beat eggs; stir in water, sweetened condensed milk, vanilla, and salt. Pour into caramelized pan; set in large pan. Fill pan with 1 inch of hot water. Bake at 350 degrees for 55 to 60 minutes. Cool. Chill thoroughly. Loosen side of flan with knife; invert onto serving plate with rim. Garnish as desired. Refrigerate leftovers.

Scotchies

1 cup flour
½ teaspoon baking soda
½ teaspoon salt
½ cup shortening
1 cup brown sugar

1 egg
1 teaspoon vanilla
½ cup pecans, chopped
1 cup quick-cooking oats
1 cup coconut (shredded or flaked)

In a small bowl, sift flour, baking soda, and salt; set aside. In a large bowl, cream shortening and beat in sugar. Add egg and vanilla, beating until light and fluffy. Stir in flour mixture, pecans, oats, and coconut. Drop by teaspoonfuls onto greased cookie sheets. Flatten each cookie with the bottom of a glass dipped in flour or sugar. Bake at 325 degrees for 12 to 15 minutes. Remove from sheet immediately. Makes about 4 dozen.

Gingerbread Cut-Out Cookies

1 cup shortening
1 cup sugar
1 egg
1 cup molasses
2 tablespoons vinegar
5 cups flour

1½ teaspoons baking soda
½ teaspoon salt
1 tablespoon ginger
1 teaspoon cinnamon
1 teaspoon cloves

In a large bowl, cream shortening with sugar. Add egg, molasses, and vinegar. Beat well. Sift dry ingredients. Stir into creamed mixture. Chill for 3 hours. Roll onto floured surface; cut with cookie cutters. Bake on ungreased cookie sheets at 375 degrees for 5 to 6 minutes.

Festive Nesselrode Pudding

3 envelopes unflavored gelatin
1 cup sugar, divided
¼ teaspoon salt
3 cups milk
5 eggs, separated
1 teaspoon vanilla
1 tablespoon rum extract
⅓ cup blanched almonds,
    chopped

⅓ cup raisins, chopped
⅓ cup dates, chopped
¼ cup citron, diced
¾ cup halved candied cherries
2 cups heavy cream, whipped,
    divided
1½ dozen ladyfingers, split
Whole cherries, citron,
    and green leaves

In a double boiler, mix gelatin, ½ cup sugar, and salt. Add milk and egg yolks; beat with whisk until blended. Place over simmering water and cook, stirring constantly, until mixture thickens and coats a metal spoon. Remove from heat and stir in flavorings. Chill until thickened, but not firm. Beat egg whites until almost stiff. Gradually add remaining sugar and beat until stiff. Fold nuts, fruits, and 1½ cups whipped cream into gelatin mixture. Pour into 9-inch springform pan lined with ladyfingers. Chill several hours. After removing from mold, decorate with remaining whipped cream, cherries, citron, and leaves.

Anise Sticks

4½ cups brown sugar
1 pint boiling water
1 heaping cup melted butter
2 teaspoons baking soda

5 teaspoons anise oil
2 teaspoons salt
1 teaspoon vanilla
10 to 12 cups flour

In a large saucepan, combine brown sugar and water and cook for 15 minutes. Cool slightly; add butter, baking soda, oil, salt, and vanilla. Stir in flour. Let stand in covered bowl for 1 hour. Using hands, roll long ropes about as thick as a pencil. Place on greased baking sheet. Bake at 375 degrees 10 to 12 minutes, or until nicely browned.

Christmas Rice Pudding

1¾ cups uncooked long grain rice
2 cups water
4 cups milk
1 cup sugar

1 teaspoon salt
¼ cup butter or margarine
Cinnamon (optional)

In a saucepan, combine rice and water. Simmer 10 minutes; add milk and bring to a boil. Reduce heat and simmer, uncovered, for 60 to 70 minutes, or until rice is tender, stirring often. Add sugar, salt, and butter. Mix well; cool. Sprinkle cinnamon on while still warm.

Spicy Walnut Raisin Pie

2 eggs
½ cup sugar
¼ cup butter or margarine
¼ teaspoon cinnamon
¼ teaspoon cloves

¼ teaspoon nutmeg
¾ cup corn syrup
Dash of salt
⅓ cup raisins
⅓ cup walnuts
Unbaked piecrust

Beat together first 8 ingredients. Stir in raisins and walnuts; pour into piecrust.
Bake at 350 degrees for 45 minutes.

Gingerbread

1½ cups flour
2 teaspoons baking soda
½ teaspoon salt
1 teaspoon cinnamon
1½ teaspoons ginger
¼ teaspoon cloves
½ teaspoon dry mustard

½ teaspoon pepper
½ cup butter or margarine,
    softened
½ cup dark brown sugar
2 eggs
1 cup molasses
1 cup boiling water

In a medium bowl, combine flour, baking soda, salt, cinnamon, ginger, cloves, mustard, and pepper. Set aside. In a large bowl, beat butter and sugar; add eggs and beat well, then beat in molasses. Add the boiling water and dry ingredients; beat until batter is smooth. Pour into a greased and floured 8x11-inch baking pan. Bake at 375 degrees for 35 to 45 minutes or until a knife inserted comes out clean.

Kiffel with Sour Cream

4 cups flour
½ teaspoon salt
1 cake yeast (2 may be used)
1¼ to 1½ cups shortening
   (butter, margarine, shortening,
   or lard—best with part lard)

½ cup sour cream
4 or 5 egg yolks, beaten
1 large orange rind, grated
Flour
Powdered sugar

Filling:
4 cups walnuts, coarsely ground
1 cup sugar
½ cup milk
2 ounces butter or margarine,
   melted

2 teaspoons vanilla
1 teaspoon almond (a little
   lemon juice may be added)

Topping:
Egg whites
Sugar

Combine flour and salt. Blend yeast well into flour mixture. Rub with hands. Cut in shortening until well mixed; stir in orange rind. Add sour cream to egg yolks, and then add to flour mixture. Knead until hands are clean. Divide into 8 or 10 balls; cover and chill overnight. On surface coated with flour and powdered sugar, roll each ball into a 9-inch circle. Cut into eighths and fill with filling (about one teaspoon on each crescent). Roll up, starting at wide end. Brush with egg whites; sprinkle with sugar. Bake on greased cookie sheets at 325 degrees for 30 minutes.

Red Velvet Cake

½ cup butter, softened
1½ cups sugar
2 eggs
1 ounce red food coloring
2½ cups flour
1 teaspoon salt

2 tablespoons cocoa
1 cup buttermilk
1 teaspoon vanilla
1 teaspoon baking soda
1 tablespoon vinegar

In a large bowl, cream butter and sugar. Add eggs and red food coloring. Mix well. In a separate bowl, combine flour, salt, and cocoa. Alternately add to creamed mixture with buttermilk. Beat after each addition. Add vanilla; mix well. Mix together baking soda and vinegar and add to mixture; mix. Pour into two 9-inch greased and floured pans. Bake at 350 degrees for 30 minutes.

Date Cake

1½ cups boiling water
1 cup chopped dates
1¾ teaspoons baking soda, divided
½ cup butter or margarine
1¼ cups sugar
2 eggs

1 cup whole wheat flour
1 cup all-purpose flour
¾ teaspoon salt
1 cup chocolate chips
½ cup brown sugar
½ cup nuts, chopped

Pour boiling water over dates and 1 teaspoon baking soda. Allow mixture to cool to room temperature. In a large bowl, cream together butter and sugar. Add eggs, then add date mixture. Stir in flours, ¾ teaspoon baking soda, and salt. Beat well until smooth. Pour into a greased oblong cake pan. Combine chocolate chips, brown sugar, and nuts, and spoon over the top of the cake batter. Bake at 325 degrees for 45 minutes.

Swedish Tarta

2 eggs
⅔ cup sugar, plus extra
   for topping
⅔ cup flour

Any fruit, such as apples,
   peaches, or blueberries,
   divided
½ cup butter, melted

Cream eggs, sugar, and flour until fluffy, and pour into a greased 9-inch round cake pan. Add fruit in a circular fashion, reserving a little for topping. Over fruit, pour melted butter, and sprinkle with sugar to form a thin top crust as it bakes. (Use cinnamon-sugar mixture for apples.) Bake at 350 degrees for 40 minutes. Top with fresh fruit.

Spritz

2 cups butter (no substitutes)
1 cup sugar
1 egg, well beaten

1 teaspoon vanilla
1 teaspoon almond extract
4 cups flour

Mix ingredients in order listed; chill dough for at least 1 hour. Put into a cookie press and press onto an ungreased cookie sheet. Bake at 400 degrees for about 10 minutes or until slightly browned. Cookies burn easily, so watch carefully. Decorate with sprinkles as desired.

Yugoslavian Christmas Cookies

1 cup butter, softened
1½ cups sugar, divided
1 egg yolk
¼ to ½ teaspoon salt
2½ cups flour

4 egg whites
¾ cup finely ground walnuts
1 teaspoon lemon extract
1 cup blackberry or currant
    jelly
1 cup chopped walnuts

In a large bowl, cream butter with ½ cup sugar; beat until fluffy. Add egg yolk and salt. Stir in flour. Pat dough into a thin layer in the bottom of a 10x15-inch cookie sheet or 9x13-inch baking pan. Beat egg whites until stiff; gradually add remaining sugar. Continue beating until it is the consistency of meringue. Fold in the ground walnuts and lemon extract. Spread jelly over dough. Swirl meringue over jelly and sprinkle with chopped walnuts. Bake at 350 degrees for 40 to 45 minutes. Cut into squares. Makes 3 to 4 dozen.

Krom Kakar

1 cup sugar
3 eggs
3 egg yolks, well beaten
1 cup cream
½ cup butter, melted

1 cup flour
½ teaspoon vanilla
½ teaspoon lemon juice
Powdered sugar (optional)

In a large bowl, mix sugar, eggs, and egg yolks; beat well. Heat both sides of a Krom Kakar iron (purchase in a Scandinavian cookware shop). Add remaining ingredients except powdered sugar; beat well. Very lightly oil or grease the iron (only once). Pour on a small amount of batter, about the size of a walnut. Close iron to bake on both sides at once. Check after 1 to 2 minutes, as cookies burn easily. When done, open the iron and use a fork to pick off the flat cookie; roll it quickly on the metal tube. Store in an airtight container. If desired, sprinkle with powdered sugar before serving. Makes 20 cookies.

Eggnog Pie

½ box gingersnap cookies, crushed
½ cup butter or margarine, softened
1 cup sugar, divided
1 envelope unflavored gelatin
½ teaspoon salt
3 eggs, separated

1¼ cups milk
¼ teaspoon cream of tartar
½ cup whipping cream, chilled
2 drops yellow food coloring
Nutmeg to taste

To make crust, mix gingersnaps and butter. Press mixture firmly and evenly against sides and bottom of a 9-inch pie pan. Bake at 350 degrees for 10 minutes; cool. To make filling, mix ½ cup sugar, gelatin, and salt in a saucepan. Mix egg yolks and milk; stir into sugar mixture. Heat over medium heat, stirring constantly until boiling. Cover and refrigerate several hours, until thickened. Beat egg whites and cream of tartar until foamy. Beat in remaining ½ cup sugar 1 tablespoon at a time. Beat until stiff and glossy; do not overbeat. Fold cooled egg mixture into meringue. Beat cream in a chilled bowl until stiff. Fold into egg mixture. Pour filling into cooled pie shell and sprinkle with nutmeg. Refrigerate until set, at least 3 hours.

Cranberry Mince Pie

⅔ cup sugar
2 tablespoons cornstarch
⅔ cup + 2 tablespoons water,
  divided
1½ cups fresh cranberries,
  rinsed and drained

1 pint homemade or
  purchased mincemeat
Pastry for 2-crust pie
1 egg yolk
Whipped cream

In a saucepan, combine sugar and cornstarch; add ⅔ cup water. Cook and stir over high heat to boiling. Add berries; bring to a boil. Reduce heat and simmer for 5 to 10 minutes, stirring occasionally. Pour mincemeat into pie crust and top with berries. Cover with vented crust. Mix egg yolk with 2 tablespoons water; brush egg wash over top of crust. Bake in lower half of oven at 425 degrees for 30 minutes. Cool; serve with real whipped cream.

Time Zone–Defying Brunch Ideas

The Son of God became man to enable
men to become the sons of God.

C. S. LEWIS

Finnish Coffee Cake

1½ cups sugar
1 cup oil
1 teaspoon vanilla
2 cups flour
½ teaspoon baking soda

1 cup milk
1 teaspoon baking powder
½ teaspoon salt
1 tablespoon cinnamon
4 tablespoons brown sugar

Glaze:
1 cup powdered sugar
½ teaspoon vanilla

1 to 2 tablespoons water

In a large bowl, beat sugar, oil, and vanilla. Add next 5 ingredients; mix well. In another bowl, mix cinnamon and brown sugar. Pour half of batter into a greased 9x13-inch cake pan. Sprinkle half of cinnamon mixture on top. Repeat layers. Bake at 350 degrees for 30 minutes. Prepare the glaze. Punch holes in cake with a fork and drizzle glaze on top. Serve warm.

Swedish Pancakes

4 eggs, separated
1½ tablespoons sugar
1¾ cups milk
1 cup sifted flour

1 teaspoon baking powder
¼ teaspoon salt
¼ teaspoon butter or
   margarine, melted

In a bowl, beat egg whites until stiff but not dry. In another bowl, mix egg yolks, sugar, milk, flour, baking powder, salt, and butter. Fold in egg whites. Heat griddle; brush lightly with grease. Pour onto griddle. Fry on both sides until golden brown. Serve with maple syrup.

French Breakfast Muffins

⅓ cup shortening
½ cup sugar
1 egg
1½ cups flour
1½ teaspoons baking powder
½ teaspoon salt

¼ teaspoon nutmeg
½ cup milk
½ cup sugar
1 teaspoon cinnamon
½ cup butter, melted

In a large bowl, mix shortening, sugar, and egg. Stir in the flour, baking powder, salt, and nutmeg. Add milk and mix well. Fill 15 greased muffin cups ⅔ full. Bake 20 to 25 minutes at 350 degrees. In a separate bowl, mix sugar and cinnamon together. Immediately after baking, roll puffs in melted butter, then in cinnamon and sugar mixture.

Christmas Wreath Coffee Cake

1½ cups sifted flour
2½ teaspoons baking powder
½ teaspoon salt
1 egg, slightly beaten

¾ cup sugar
⅓ cup melted shortening
½ cup milk
1 teaspoon vanilla

Streusel:
½ cup brown sugar, firmly packed
2 tablespoons flour

¾ teaspoon cinnamon
2 teaspoons shortening

Glaze:
1 tablespoon milk
1 cup powdered sugar, sifted

½ teaspoon vanilla

In a large bowl, sift together flour, baking power, and salt. In a separate bowl, combine remaining ingredients. Stir into flour mixture, just until blended. Set aside. For streusel, combine brown sugar, flour, and cinnamon. Cut in shortening until crumbly. Place half of streusel in greased 1-quart ring mold; top with half of batter. Repeat layers. Bake at 375 degrees for about 30 minutes. Cool 10 minutes in mold; invert on wire rack. Cool. Combine glaze ingredients; stir to blend well. Drizzle over cake.

Norwegian Coffee Cake

4 cups flour
6 teaspoons baking powder
1 cup sugar
½ teaspoon salt
1 cup butter or margarine

2 eggs
1 cup milk
Frosting
Chopped nuts

In a large bowl, sift together dry ingredients. Blend in butter as for pie crust. In a separate bowl, beat eggs and milk. Add to dry ingredients, being careful not to overmix. Grease two 9-inch cake pans and put half of mixture in each pan by putting spoonfuls around the edge. Bake at 400 degrees for 20 minutes. Frost and add nuts to the top.

Individual Quiches

Pastry for 2-crust pie
¾ cup chopped cooked shrimp,
 bacon, or crab
4 ounces Swiss cheese, shredded
¼ sliced green onion

½ cup mayonnaise
2 eggs
⅓ cup milk
¼ teaspoon salt
¼ teaspoon dill weed

On floured surface, roll half of the pastry. Cut circles to size of muffin pan. Repeat for 6 more. Fit in 12 2½-inch muffin cups. Fill each with shrimp, bacon, or crab; cheese; and onion. Beat together remaining ingredients and divide into 12 cups. Bake at 350 degrees, until well browned.

Dutch Potato Pancakes

4 cups mashed potatoes
3 tablespoons flour
2 eggs, lightly beaten

1 tablespoon baking powder
Pinch of salt
1 cup milk

Mix together all ingredients. Beat into batter. Pour onto hot, greased griddle. Fry on both sides until golden brown.

Breakfast Sausage Hot Dish

2½ cups herbed croutons
2 cups medium sharp cheese, shredded
2 pounds ground sausage
4 eggs, beaten

¾ teaspoon dry mustard
2½ cups milk
1 can cream of mushroom soup
1 small can mushroom pieces

Place croutons in greased 8x10-inch baking dish. Top with cheese. Cook sausage in skillet until brown. Drain on paper towel. Place sausage over cheese. Beat eggs; mix in mustard, milk, mushroom soup, and mushroom pieces. Pour over sausage. Bake at 300 degrees for 90 minutes. Serves 8.

*Note: This can be made ahead of time and refrigerated overnight.

Overnight French Toast

½ cup pecans, chopped
1 cup + 1 tablespoon brown sugar
½ cup butter
2 tablespoons non-maple
  pancake syrup

12 slices white bread
6 eggs, beaten
1½ cups milk
1 teaspoon vanilla
½ teaspoon salt

Spray a 9x13-inch baking dish with cooking spray; sprinkle pecans evenly over the bottom of the pan. Set aside. In a saucepan, combine brown sugar, butter, and syrup and cook until thick; pour mixture over the pecans. Place 6 slices of bread on top of the mixture. Stack remaining 6 slices over the first layer. Combine eggs, milk, vanilla, and salt. Pour over the bread slices. Refrigerate 8 hours or overnight. Bake at 350 degrees for 40 to 45 minutes.

German Oven Pancake

½ cup flour
3 eggs, slightly beaten
½ cup milk
2 tablespoons butter or
  margarine, melted

½ teaspoon salt
Melted butter
Powdered sugar

Gradually add flour to eggs; whisk. Stir in milk, butter, and salt. Grease a 9- or 10-inch ovenproof skillet or pie pan. Pour batter into cold skillet. Bake at 450 degrees for 20 minutes. Brush with melted butter and sprinkle with powdered sugar. Serve immediately.

Apple Cream Scones

2 cups tart apples, chopped
6 tablespoons butter, divided
1 tablespoon instant coffee crystals
1 teaspoon hot water
½ cup whipped topping

2¼ cups flour
⅓ cup sugar
1 tablespoon baking powder
¼ teaspoon salt
2 tablespoons coarse sugar

In a saucepan, cook apples in 2 tablespoons butter until tender and liquid is almost evaporated, stirring often; cool slightly. In a small bowl, dissolve coffee in water and stir in whipped topping. In a large bowl, mix flour, ⅓ cup sugar, baking powder, and salt; cut in remaining butter until pieces resemble coarse crumbs. Add apples and coffee mixture; stir just until dough clings together.

On a lightly floured surface, knead dough 6 times. On ungreased baking sheet, pat dough into 8-inch circle. Top with coarse sugar. Cut into 8 or 10 wedges; separate slightly. Bake at 400 degrees for 20 to 25 minutes, or until done. Cool slightly; serve warm.

Stuffed French Toast

1 to 2 bananas
1 apple
1 pear
¼ cup pecans, chopped
¼ cup brown sugar
2 eggs
1½ cups milk

½ cup flour
1 teaspoon cinnamon
½ teaspoon nutmeg
⅛ teaspoon cloves
4 tablespoons butter
1 French bread loaf, thickly
   sliced

Peel fruit; thinly slice. Combine fruit and nuts in a bowl; sprinkle with brown sugar. In another bowl, beat eggs and next 5 ingredients until creamy. Cut each slice of bread to back edge (not through); open slices and spread evenly with butter. Fill slices evenly with fruit mixture, pressing halves together to seal. Dip stuffed slices in batter and cook on griddle until lightly browned on both sides.

Swiss and Crab Quiche

6 ounces Swiss cheese, shredded
1 (9 inch) unbaked pie shell
8 ounces crab meat
2 green onions, sliced
3 eggs, beaten

1 cup light cream
½ teaspoon salt
½ teaspoon grated lemon peel
¼ teaspoon dry mustard

Arrange cheese evenly over bottom of pie shell. Top with crab meat. Sprinkle with onions. Combine eggs, cream, salt, lemon peel, and dry mustard. Pour evenly over crab meat. Top with remaining cheese. Bake at 325 degrees for 45 minutes or until set. Remove from oven and let stand 10 minutes before serving. Serves 6.

Crustless Quiche

8 ounces Swiss or mozzarella cheese,
   grated
5 to 6 slices bacon, fried and crumbled
1 cup chopped ham
10 ounces chopped broccoli
1 (7 ounce) can sliced mushrooms,
   drained
4 unbeaten eggs

½ cup onion, chopped
1½ cups milk
½ cup flour
2 tablespoons butter or
   margarine (optional)
½ teaspoon salt
Dash pepper

Sprinkle cheese into a greased 10-inch pie plate. Top with crumbled bacon, ham, broccoli, and mushrooms. Put remaining ingredients in blender; blend for 1 minute. Pour over ingredients in pie plate. Bake for 35 minutes at 350 degrees. If using a glass pie plate, quiche may need to cook longer. Let stand 3 to 4 minutes before serving.

Turkish Pancakes

4 eggs, slightly beaten
1½ cups flour
½ teaspoon salt

1½ cups milk
¼ cup butter

In a bowl, beat eggs; gradually add flour, salt, and milk. Melt butter in a 9x13-inch baking dish. Pour batter over butter. Bake at 400 degrees for 30 minutes.

The Second Time Around

*The purpose and cause of the incarnation was that
He might illuminate the world by His wisdom
and excite it to the love of Himself.*

PETER ABELARD

Day-After Turkey Divan

1 (10 ounce) package frozen broccoli
8 large slices cooked turkey
1 (10 ounce) can cream of
    mushroom soup

⅓ cup milk
½ cup cheddar cheese,
    shredded

Cook broccoli until it is almost done. Drain well; place in a shallow baking dish. Top with turkey slices. Blend soup and milk; pour over turkey. Sprinkle with cheese. Bake at 450 degrees for 15 minutes, or until lightly browned. Serves 8.

Mexican Turkey Roll-Ups

2½ cups cooked turkey, cubed
1½ cups sour cream, divided
3 teaspoons taco seasoning, divided
1 can cream of mushroom soup,
    divided
1½ cups cheddar cheese, shredded,
    divided

1 small onion, chopped
½ cup salsa
¼ cup sliced olives
10 flour tortillas
Shredded lettuce
Chopped tomatoes
Additional salsa (optional)

In a large bowl, combine turkey, ½ cup sour cream, 1½ teaspoons taco seasoning, ½ of the soup, 1 cup cheese, onion, ½ cup salsa, and olives. Spoon ⅓ cup filling onto each tortilla. Roll up; place seam side down in a greased 9x13-inch baking dish. Combine remaining sour cream, taco seasoning, and soup; pour over tortillas. Cover and bake at 350 degrees for 30 minutes. Sprinkle with remaining cheese. Serve with shredded lettuce and chopped tomatoes, and top with salsa. Serves 5.

Turkey Cordon Bleu

¾ pound cooked turkey, cut into strips
¼ pound boiled ham, cut into strips
2 tablespoons butter
1 (10 ounce) can cream
  of chicken soup
1 cup water

2 tablespoons Dijon
  mustard (optional)
1 (10 ounce) package
  cut green beans
1½ cups minute rice
8 ounces Swiss cheese, cubed

In a saucepan, cook and stir turkey and ham in hot butter until lightly browned.
Stir in soup, water, and mustard; add green beans. Bring to a full boil. Stir in rice
and top with cheese. Cover; remove from heat. Let stand 5 minutes. Fluff with
fork.

Ham and Green Bean Pie

1½ cups fully cooked smoked ham, chopped
1 (9 ounce) package green beans, rinsed and drained
1 (4½ ounce) jar sliced mushrooms

1 cup Swiss cheese, shredded
1½ cups milk
3 eggs
¾ cup baking mix

Sprinkle ham, beans, mushrooms, and cheese in a greased 10-inch pie plate. Beat remaining ingredients until smooth, using a blender for approximately 15 seconds or a hand mixer for 1 minute. Add to pie plate. Bake at 400 degrees 40 to 45 minutes, until knife inserted in center comes out clean. Cool 5 minutes. Serves 6 to 8.

Turkey Casserole

1 (4 ounce) can sliced mushrooms,
   drained (reserve liquid)
⅓ cup onion, chopped
¾ cup butter or margarine
3 tablespoons flour
¾ teaspoon salt
Dash pepper
3 cups milk and mushroom
   liquid (combined total)

2 cups cooked turkey, cubed
1 (8 ounce) package egg
   noodles
Grated Parmesan cheese
½ cup bread crumbs
2 tablespoons butter
   or margarine

In a large saucepan, sauté mushrooms and onion in butter until crisp-tender. Blend in flour and seasonings. Add milk and mushroom liquid. Cook, stirring constantly, until sauce thickens. Add turkey. Meanwhile, cook noodles according to package directions; drain in colander. Combine noodles with sauce in 2-quart casserole. Top with Parmesan cheese and bread crumbs tossed with butter. Bake at 400 degrees for 20 to 25 minutes, or until browned. Serves 6.

Ham and Broccoli Casserole

2 (10 ounce) packages frozen
  chopped broccoli
2 cups fully cooked ham, cubed
1½ cups cheddar cheese, shredded

1 cup baking mix
3 cups milk
4 eggs

Cook broccoli according to package directions; drain. Spread in ungreased 9x13-inch pan. Layer ham and cheese over broccoli. Beat remaining ingredients until smooth. Slowly pour over cheese. Bake at 350 degrees for 1 hour uncovered.

Turkey Pot Pie

1 (6 ounce) package chicken-flavored
  stuffing mix
¼ cup butter or margarine,
  cut into pieces
1½ cups hot water

1 can cream of chicken soup
1 cup milk
3 cups turkey, cut up
1 package frozen mixed
  vegetables

Place contents of vegetable/seasoning mix and butter in a bowl. Add water and stir to partially melt butter. Add stuffing cubes and stir gently. Mix soup and milk in 2-quart casserole dish. Stir in turkey and vegetables. Spoon stuffing over turkey mixture. Bake at 350 degrees for 45 minutes or until hot and bubbly.

INDEX